I0189805

JOSEPH and JONAH

A Faithful Servant and a Runaway Preacher

Sarah Jane Conaway

Copyright © 2019 Joseph and Jonah

A Faithful Servant and a Runaway Preacher

All rights reserved.

No part of this publication may be reproduced, distributed, or transmitted in any form or by any means, including photocopying, recording, or other electronic or mechanical methods, without the prior written permission of the publisher, except in the case of brief quotations embodied in reviews and certain other non-commercial uses permitted by copyright law.

First Printing 2019

First Edition 2019

10 9 8 7 6 5 4 3 2 1

Dedication

This book is dedicated to the reader.
I pray that you increase your knowledge of
the Word of God in your study of this book.

Table of Contents

JONAH

Introduction

Several years ago I began writing lessons for my ladies' classes inspired by questions in the Bible. In April 2015 the Lord touched my heart to put these lessons in book form. I embarked on this new phase of my ministry with overwhelming feelings. As a result, in my first edition of this book, I was impressed to disclose only a few lessons.

This book is based on two men. One was obedient to the Lord and kept his faith in Him, even though things were going very wrong. He never held a grudge. He always did his best. This man's name is Joseph. You will see how he stayed faithful to the Lord in spite of his circumstances. The other man, Jonah, was already a preacher. He refused to do what the Lord told him, so he ran away. You will see how the Lord's will was done even though both men were so different.

My prayer is that these lessons will whet your appetite to dig deeper into the Word of God and study more about these men. There is so much that I have not written, but the purpose is to give you an appetizer, making you want to know more. So that you will study some area in deeper thought in order to get your own message from our Lord and Saviour.

All Scripture references are from the King James Bible. All emphases are from this author.

Be blessed in your study,

JOSEPH AND JONAH

Sarah Jane Conaway
The Author
sarahjane@auntjane.ws
www.amazon.com/author/sarahjane

JOSEPH

CHAPTER 1

The Child Is Not;
And I, Whither Shall I Go?

Genesis 37

Joseph's story concerns the things that happened to him because of jealousy and hatred. Many questions arise in this lesson that are significant to the story. Let's start reading in Genesis 37:1-3.

> *¹And Jacob dwelt in the land wherein his father was a stranger, in the land of Canaan. ² These are the generations of Jacob. Joseph, being seventeen years old, was feeding the flock with his brethren; and the lad was with the sons of Bilhah, and with the sons of Zilpah, his father's wives: and Joseph brought unto his father their evil report. ³ Now Israel loved Joseph more than all his children, because he was the son of his old age: and he made him a coat of many colours.*

In these first three verses we have the making of problems within the family. First, 17 year-old Joseph would run to his daddy and tattle on his brothers when they did wrong or disobeyed. Secondly, to add to this picture, Jacob loved Joseph more than his other sons. He had ten sons before he had Joseph. Jacob was so excited that his beloved Rachel had given him a son. She had been barren for so many years. He loved this boy born in his old age. Jacob made Joseph a coat of many colors. We are going to see what this did to the ten older brothers. Let's read verses 4-7.

> *⁴ And when his brethren saw that their father loved him more than all his brethren, they hated him, and could not speak peaceably unto him. ⁵ And Joseph dreamed a dream, and he told it his brethren: and they hated him yet the more. ⁶ And he said unto them, Hear, I pray you, this dream which I have dreamed: ⁷ For, behold, we were binding sheaves in the field, and, lo, my sheaf arose, and also stood upright; and, behold, your sheaves stood round about, and made obeisance to my sheaf.*

All of the older brothers hated Joseph because they saw more love given to him from their father than to them. They blamed Joseph rather than their father. They hated him so much that they could not even talk kindly to him. The dreams that Joseph dreamed indicated that he would rule over them someday. This made matters worse. These men were in their 20s & 30s maybe even older. They could not believe that this kid would really reign over them. They were irritated that he could believe this could possibly come to be. Let's read the next few verses.

> *⁸And his brethren said to him, Shalt thou indeed reign over us? or shalt thou indeed have dominion over us? And they hated him yet the more for his dreams, and for his words. ⁹And he dreamed yet another dream, and told it his brethren, and said, Behold, I have dreamed a dream more; and, behold, the sun and the moon and the eleven stars made obeisance to me.¹⁰And he told it to his father, and to his brethren: and his father rebuked him, and said unto him,* **What is this dream that thou hast dreamed? Shall I and thy mother and thy brethren indeed come to bow down ourselves to thee to the earth?** *¹¹And his brethren envied him; but his father observed the saying.*

When Joseph told them about the dream of the sun, moon and eleven stars bowing to his star, his brothers resented him. We have the first question of consideration for this lesson. Jacob is questioning his 17-year old son. "What are you talking about? Do you really think that your mother and I and your brothers will actually bow to you?" Jacob's anger rose against Joseph, yet Jacob thought about what these dreams should really mean.

One day Jacob sent Joseph to see how the brothers were getting along. Joseph arrived at the field where they should be feeding the flock, but none of his brothers or the herd were anywhere in sight. Then a man asked Joseph, **"What seekest thou?"** Joseph said that he was looking for his brothers. The man told Joseph that they said that they should go to Dothan. Joseph found them in Dothan. Let's read what the brothers were saying when they saw him coming. Read verses 18-20.

> *18 And when they saw him afar off, even before he came near unto them, they conspired against him to slay him. 19 And they said one to another, Behold, this dreamer cometh. 20 Come now therefore, and let us slay him, and cast him into some pit, and we will say, Some evil beast hath devoured him: and we shall see what will become of his dreams.*

Now we know that they were so full of hate that they wanted to kill their little brother. In planning to commit the sin of murder, they were also planning how to explain it to their father. So that means they had to add another sin to their list of sins—lying. One of the brothers did not like what he heard. Read verses 21-22.

> *21 And Reuben heard it, and he delivered him out of their hands; and said, Let us not kill him. 22 And Reuben said unto them, Shed no blood, but cast him into this pit that is in the wilderness, and lay no hand upon him; that he might rid him out of their hands, to deliver him to his father again.*

Reuben had his own plan. He wanted to return the boy to his father so he said, "Don't kill him, just put him in this pit." Reuben planned to go for the boy later and take him back to his father. Continue with verses 23-24.

[23] And it came to pass, when Joseph was come unto his brethren, that they stript Joseph out of his coat, his coat of many colours that was on him; [24] And they took him, and cast him into a pit: and the pit was empty, there was no water in it.

They pulled the special coat off Joseph. They knew that this would be the best way to identify him. They lowered Joseph into a dry well. They ignored all of the cries and questions that Joseph put to them. They wanted this dreamer, this nuisance of a little brother out of mind and sight, but murder and lying were not the right way to take care of their problem. Let's read verses 25-28.

[25] And they sat down to eat bread: and they lifted up their eyes and looked, and, behold, a company of Ishmeelites came from Gilead with their camels bearing spicery and balm and myrrh, going to carry it down to Egypt. [26] And Judah said unto his brethren, **What profit is it if we slay our brother, and conceal his blood?** *[27] Come, and let us sell him to the Ishmeelites, and let not our hand be upon him; for he is our brother and our flesh. And his brethren were content. [28] Then there passed by Midianites merchantmen; and they drew and lifted up Joseph out of the pit, and sold Joseph to the Ishmeelites for twenty pieces of silver: and they brought Joseph into Egypt.*

After dropping Joseph into the deep, dry well, they sat down to eat. Judah poses a question "**What profit is it if we slay our brother, and conceal his blood?"** Then he came up with a plan. "Hey, let's not kill him; let's just sell him as a slave. After all he is our little brother and we don't really want to hurt him." So, Joseph was sold and his Ishmeelite owners took him into Egypt. Reuben was not present when this took place. Read verses 29-32.

> [29] *And Reuben returned unto the pit; and, behold, Joseph was not in the pit; and he rent his clothes.* [30] *And he returned unto his brethren, and said,* **The child is not; and I, whither shall I go?** [31] *And they took Joseph's coat, and killed a kid of the goats, and dipped the coat in the blood;* [32] *And they sent the coat of many colours, and they brought it to their father; and said, This have we found: know now whether it be thy son's coat or no.*

When Reuben rejoined his family, he went straight to the old well to rescue Joseph, but when he looked over the edge of the well, it was empty! He cried out, "**The child is not; and I, whither shall I go?** (Genesis 37:30) In other words, he was saying, "How can I go back to our father without Joseph? How can I face our father? It will bring him so much grief." The brothers continued to use the plan that they made to explain it away to their father. They showed the coat to him and said, "Is this your son's coat?" Continue reading verses 33-35.

10

³³ And he knew it, and said, It is my son's coat; an evil beast hath devoured him; Joseph is without doubt rent in pieces. ³⁴ And Jacob rent his clothes, and put sackcloth upon his loins, and mourned for his son many days. ³⁵ And all his sons and all his daughters rose up to comfort him; but he refused to be comforted; and he said, For I will go down into the grave unto my son mourning. Thus his father wept for him.

Jacob knew immediately that it was Joseph's coat. He saw the familiar material that he had so lovingly woven into a coat for his beloved son. He assumed that an animal had killed Joseph. He went into grieving, a grief that was to last a very long time. The sins of these grown men caused an abundance of grief to their father as well as to their little brother. Let's name these sins:

Hatred, Jealousy, and Lying are just for starters. One sin festers and continues to create more sin.

Joseph was very much alive. The Midianites sold him to Potiphar. Joseph had now become a slave in Egypt. Remember he was only 17 years-old. What a sad thing to happen to a teenager.

What can we learn from this story? The brothers let their hatred and jealousy direct their actions. Jacob, also, had deep-seated anger and as a result showed preferential treatment to one son. We need to recognize in our own lives the sin that is there and deal with it. We must do this regardless of whether or not others take care of their sin. Reuben attempted to do this. He desired to return the boy to his father. I don't believe any of them really realized just how hard this would be on their father. When we acknowledge the sin that is in our lives and confess it to the Lord, we need to follow His leading to correct it.

1 John 1:9 says,
If we confess our sins, he is faithful and just to forgive us our sins, and to cleanse us from all unrighteousness.

- **Don't let sin reign in your life.**

- **Agree with God about it immediately.**

Homework:

1. Memorize 1 John 1:9.

2. To the Christian, examine your own life to see if there is hidden resentment or any other sin. Take the necessary steps to cleanse your life, to draw yourself closer to the Lord, to renew your fellowship with Him. Write about how this has changed your thinking, your speaking and your everyday actions.

3. To the lost person, accept Jesus' payment for sin for yourself. Ask a Christian friend or pastor to help you.

4. Any of you are welcome to contact me for help – sarahjane@auntjane.ws

NOTES

NOTES

NOTES

CHAPTER 2

How Then Can I Do This Great Wickedness, And Sin Against God?

Genesis 39

The story of Joseph continues. We can't just leave him as a slave. We need to learn from Joseph. I imagine that he learned from his own mistakes as well.

Joseph is in Potiphar's house. He is a slave. He has his day planned for him by someone else. He has no control over that. However, he did have control over how he responded to this servitude. Let's read Genesis 39:2-5.

² And the Lord was with Joseph, and he was a prosperous man; and he was in the house of his master the Egyptian. ³ And his master saw that the Lord was with him, and that the Lord made all that he did to prosper in his hand. ⁴ And Joseph found grace in his sight, and he served him: and he made him overseer over his house, and all that he had he put into his hand. ⁵ And it came to pass from the time that he had made him overseer in his house, and over all that he had, that the Lord blessed the Egyptian's house for Joseph's sake; and the blessing of the Lord was upon all that he had in the house, and in the field.

Joseph trusted in the Lord for everything. Even though he was sold as a slave, he gave his "job" all of his attention to do the best that he could. The Lord blessed him. Everything that Joseph did, blossomed and multiplied. Potiphar saw what the Lord did in this young man's life and gave him more and more responsibility. Verse 6 even states that Potiphar did not even know all that he had. He trusted Joseph completely, but here comes trouble. Read, please, verses 7-9.

[7] And it came to pass after these things, that his master's wife cast her eyes upon Joseph; and she said, Lie with me. [8] But he refused, and said unto his master's wife, Behold, my master wotteth not what is with me in the house, and he hath committed all that he hath to my hand; [9] There is none greater in this house than I; neither hath he kept back any thing from me but thee, because thou art his wife: **how then can I do this great wickedness, and sin against God?**

Joseph refused the attention that Mrs. Potiphar showered on him. He knew that it was sin and he could not sin against his master and his Lord. He realized that all of his prosperity had come from the Lord and he was not going to jeopardize it just to fulfill human desire. She continued day in and day out to tempt him, but he kept refusing. Then one day they just happened to be alone in the house and she pressed him hard and he ran from her. She grabbed his coat and Joseph left without it. Scripture tells us to flee fornication. Read 1 Corinthians 6:18,

> **Flee** *fornication. Every sin that a man doeth is without the body; but he that committeth fornication sinneth against his own body.*

It also says in James 4:7 to submit and to resist.

> **Submit** *yourselves therefore to God.*
> **Resist** *the devil, and he will flee from you.*

Joseph **submitted** to God and **fled** from sin, but that did not stop this woman. She expressed lies about Joseph to the other workers in the house and then to her husband. We can read what she said in verses 16-19.

> [16] *And she laid up his garment by her, until his lord came home.* [17] *And she spake unto him according to these words, saying, The Hebrew servant, which thou hast brought unto us, came in unto me to mock me:* [18] *And it came to pass, as I lifted up my voice and cried, that he left his garment with me, and fled out.* [19] *And it came to pass, when his master heard the words of his wife, which she spake unto him, saying, After this manner did thy servant to me; that his wrath was kindled.*

All of Joseph's hard work and dependence on the Lord **seemed** to vanish with this wicked, lying woman. He **could** have said, what's the point in following the Lord? But praise the Lord HE DID NOT SAY THAT, even though his master threw him into prison. He kept right on serving the Lord and giving whatever job he was given his best and kept his FAITH in the Lord. Let's read this in verses 21-23.

21 But the Lord was with Joseph, and shewed him mercy, and gave him favour in the sight of the keeper of the prison. 22 And the keeper of the prison committed to Joseph's hand all the prisoners that were in the prison; and whatsoever they did there, he was the doer of it. 23 The keeper of the prison looked not to any thing that was under his hand; because the Lord was with him, and that which he did, the Lord made it to prosper.

Joseph was faithful to his Lord and to what he believed. We need to learn that bad things do happen to good people. There is a verse in Psalm 34 that fits this lesson. Let's read verse 19.

Many are the afflictions of the righteous but the Lord delivereth him out of them all.

- **Be faithful to the Lord
no matter what happens in your life.**

- **He is standing with you.**

If you don't have the Lord in your life, look at what He did for you on the cross. He shed all of His blood for you to cleanse away your sin. Make a decision to believe in Him.

- **By faith trust Jesus today.**

Homework:

Memorize James 4:7 and Psalm 34:19.

Examine your life and put it in the capable hands of our Lord. Write down what area or areas you need to place into the hands of Jesus and how you will let go of the results.

NOTES

NOTES

NOTES

CHAPTER 3

Can We Find Such a
One As This Is, A Man in
Whom the Spirit of God Is?

Genesis 40-41

Joseph remained in prison, but the length of time he had been there, the Bible is not specific. Two new men were put into prison and, of course, Joseph had charge of them. One was the chief butler and the other the chief baker. After they had been there several months, they both had dreams the very same night. The next morning Joseph noticed that they were sad. Let's read what Joseph said in Genesis 40:7-8.

> *[7]And he asked Pharaoh's officers that were with him in the ward of his lord's house, saying, Wherefore look ye so sadly to day? [8]And they said unto him, We have dreamed a dream, and there is no interpreter of it. And Joseph said unto them,* **Do not interpretations belong to God?** *tell me them, I pray you.*

Joseph had sympathy for these two men. He knew that his all-knowing God could use him to help these men. The chief butler told his dream first. Joseph interpreted that he would be restored to his position in the palace. (You can read the details in Genesis 40.) When the baker saw that the interpretation for the butler was positive, he was excited to tell Joseph his dream as well. But this dream was sad. The baker was to be hanged. All of this was to happen in 3 days. Joseph asked the butler to remember him to Pharaoh because he was in prison for no real reason. Read the last three verses in this chapter to find out what happened.

²¹ And he restored the chief butler unto his butlership again; and he gave the cup into Pharaoh's hand: ²² But he hanged the chief baker: as Joseph had interpreted to them. ²³ Yet did not the chief butler remember Joseph, but forgat him.

There was a party and the butler was restored to his position of service but the baker was hung, just as Joseph had interpreted. Another sad thing happened in Joseph's life—the butler forgot to tell anyone about him. So Joseph remained in prison. Yet Joseph did not depart from his faith in God. Two more years passed and Pharaoh had a dream that no one could interpret. This was when the butler remembered Joseph. He told Pharaoh about this Hebrew who had predicted what would be the outcome of their dreams. He had lived and the baker had died.

Pharaoh immediately called for Joseph to come to him. Joseph cleaned up according to the customs of the Egyptians. He went before Pharaoh and was told the two dreams that had been dreamed. Joseph proceeded to interpret the dreams as one dream. They were to have seven years of plenty and then seven years of famine. Joseph suggested that they give one man the position of saving during the first seven years, so that they would have food in the seven years of famine. Listen to what Pharaoh says to his people in Genesis 41:38.

³⁸ And Pharaoh said unto his servants, Can we find such a one as this is, a man in whom the Spirit of God is?

What a blessing to Joseph to hear that statement made about himself! Pharaoh made Joseph second ruler in the land of Egypt. He gave him a wife and she bare him two sons. Life was so much better for Joseph. We hear often this statement, "From rags to riches." Truly, Joseph went from rags to riches in less than 24 hours. Or you could say that he went from the Prison to the Palace. Joseph knew how to suffer, and he was finding out how to abound. He never forgot his Lord. He remained faithful. There is one thing that the Bible does not mention, but I have often wondered about it. How did Potiphar and his wife respond when they had to kneel before Joseph?

It is recorded in Genesis 41:46 that Joseph was thirty years old. He became a slave when he was seventeen and now he was a ruler in Egypt at thirty. Thirteen years he suffered but now God had rewarded him for his faithfulness.

Joseph immediately puts into action the plan that he'd told Pharaoh. Life was good during the years of plenty, but the day came when the plenty was gone. We should always plan for the future in case things go south.

- **Planning and saving for the future is always a wise investment.**

If Joseph had not planned for the future, many people in Egypt and other countries would have died, maybe even his own family. We should take lessons from this story for our daily lives.

Homework:

1. Memorize: Matthew 25:21 *His lord said unto him, Well done, thou good and **faithful** servant: thou hast **been faithful** over a few things, I will make thee ruler over many things: enter thou into the joy of thy lord.*

2. Is there a way to apply this to your life? Write down three ways that this can become a practical part of your life.

NOTES

NOTES

CHAPTER 4

What Is This That God
Hath Done Unto Us?

Genesis 42-46

The prophecy of the famine came true. We find Jacob telling his sons to go to Egypt to buy food. He had heard that there was food available. Little did they know that, as they took their journey to Egypt, a surprise awaited them. They went before the ruler of Egypt that sold the supply of food. They bowed before him. Joseph remembered his dreams. He recognized his brothers, but they didn't know that the man in front of them was really their brother. Let's think about this for a moment. The last time they saw Joseph he was a seventeen-year old dreamer as they had called him. Joseph began ruling in Egypt when he was thirty. Now it was well into the time of famine. This made Joseph about thirty-eight years old. There is a big difference between a boy of seventeen and a man of thirty-eight. Also, the Egyptian men shaved themselves completely so that they had no body hair. The Israelites, on the other hand, all had beards. They would not expect this ruler to be any one they knew. Joseph accused them of being spies. He asked them questions about their family. He wanted to know of the welfare of his father and little brother. Of course, he was rough with them even putting them into lockup for three days. He kept Simeon and let the others go. Their money was returned to them in their corn sacks. They were all terrified. Note what they said in Genesis 42:28.

And he said unto his brethren, My money is restored; and, lo, it is even in my sack: and their heart failed them, and they were afraid, saying one to another, **What is this that God hath done unto us?**

Were they blaming God for what was happening to them? It had been at least 22 years since they had sold Joseph. Why would God wait that long to punish them? Hey, with God, time is irrelevant.

- **There are people alive today that are in sin.**

- **We don't see God's punishment on them, but it will come.**

They told their father all that had happened. They reluctantly told Jacob that they would have to take Benjamin with them the next time to be accepted as honest men or they would not get any food. Jacob was hovering over his youngest son in a protective manner.

This son was at least thirty years old. Yet Jacob wouldn't let Benjamin go for fear that something bad would happen to him. I can just imagine how Benjamin felt about all of this. Verse 38 explains very clearly how Jacob felt about Benjamin.

...My son shall not go down with you; for his brother is dead, and he is left alone: if mischief befall him by the way in the which ye go, then shall ye bring down my gray hairs with sorrow to the grave.

In chapter 43 the sons of Jacob finally convinced Jacob to let Benjamin go with them. His grief was beyond description. Joseph, he assumed, was dead. Simeon was in lock-up and he was fearful about what could happen to his last-born son. The ten brothers went to Egypt with presents and double money.

When Joseph saw his brothers, he commanded his servants to prepare food, so that they could eat with him. Joseph had always spoken in the Egyptian language through an interpreter. Joseph had to leave the room to hide the tears that sprang into his eyes over his younger brother. His brothers were fearful because of the special invitation. They were amazed that when they sat down to eat they were placed in their birth order. They were all given portions, but Benjamin's portion was five times more than the others.

In chapter 44 the brothers have their food and were ready to leave. Joseph gave instructions to the servant to put all the money back into their corn sacks as before and to put his silver cup in Benjamin's sack.

In verse 4 he tells his servant to go after them and ask this question,

"...Wherefore have ye rewarded evil for good?

They were accused of stealing from the ruler of Egypt. The brothers denied stealing. They had no need to steal. Read verses 9-10 to see what will happen to the man who has the silver cup.

9With whomsoever of thy servants it be found, both let him die, and we also will be my lord's bondmen. 10And he said, Now also let it be according unto your words: he with whom it is found shall be my servant; and ye shall be blameless.

Of course, the brothers didn't know that the cup was in Benjamin's sack. They were just trying to prove that they did not steal. Not one of them did. However, the cup was found in Benjamin's sack and the older brothers fell sick with fear.

Joseph was outraged with them and said that only the man with the cup will be his servant. The rest of them were allowed to go back to their father.

Judah relayed to Joseph all that happened when they got home the last time. He told how much grief their father had suffered because of the death of Benjamin's brother. Now if they go back without Benjamin the father will surely die. Judah went into detail trying to convince the ruler to change his mind. "The old man will surely die. Please don't make us go back without our little brother." Remember it was Judah that convinced the others to sell Joseph instead of killing him. He did not want to see what would happen to his father. He saw it once and that was enough.

Joseph could take no more. In chapter 45 he sends out all of the servants so that he can be alone with his brothers. Let's read verses 3-5.

³ And Joseph said unto his brethren, I AM JOSEPH; **doth my father yet live?** *And his brethren could not answer him; for they were troubled at his presence. ⁴ And Joseph said unto his brethren, Come near to me, I pray you. And they came near. And he said, I AM JOSEPH YOUR BROTHER, WHOM YE SOLD INTO EGYPT.*

Shock filled their faces! They could not believe their ears. This Egyptian man is our brother! He must be, because he knows that we sold our brother as a slave. Their fear showed in their eyes. I believe they had a right to be afraid. They had sinned against Joseph, their father and most especially against God.

What do you think Benjamin was thinking? You guys did what?! You sold my brother! He could not believe that his brothers had lied. My brother is alive! Hey, but this man is still speaking, the one who is calling himself Joseph.

> *5 Now therefore be not grieved, nor angry with yourselves, that ye sold me hither:* **for God did send me before you to preserve life.** *6 For these two years hath the famine been in the land: and yet there are five years, in the which there shall neither be earing nor harvest.* **7 And God sent me before you to preserve you a posterity in the earth, and to save your lives by a great deliverance.** *8 So now* **it was not you** *that sent me hither,* **but God:** *and he hath made me a father to Pharaoh, and lord of all his house, and a ruler throughout all the land of Egypt.*

Joseph was not blaming them for anything. He told his brothers not to be afraid or angry with themselves. God had this in His plan all along. He hugged all of his brothers and then said, "Hurry, bring my father here that I may see him."

They went back to Canaan to tell Jacob that Joseph was alive and is the ruler over Egypt! Jacob almost did not believe them, but finally he did. He was reunited with the son that he thought was dead.

In chapter 46 we see Jacob and all of his family going into Egypt. God gave Jacob permission to go. There is a list of all of his family. I think one thing is very interesting that is in verse 21. Benjamin was also the father of ten sons.

Homework:

1. Memorize Romans 8:28 *And we know that all things work together for good to them that love God, to them who are the called according to his purpose.*

2. Study the chapters thoroughly. Write down three things that stand out to you that you can apply to your own life. Include how you will put each of these into practical everyday living.

NOTES

NOTES

NOTES

CHAPTER 5

Am I In The Place Of God?

Genesis 50

We now see that over the years Joseph changed. He was no longer the teen that was boasting about his dreams and flaunting them over his brothers. He has realized that the Lord was with him all the way. I believe he learned that while in Potiphar's house before Mrs. Potiphar lied about him. Of course, that is just my opinion.

Now we are in the last chapter of Genesis. Joseph's father, Jacob, has died. Joseph grieves for his father, as do all of his brothers and their families. Joseph asks permission from Pharaoh to go to Canaan to bury Jacob in their land as his father made him promise. Pharaoh gives that permission. In fact, many of the Egyptians go along to mourn the father of the man that saved their lives from starvation. Now that Jacob has been buried, his older sons have a worry on their hearts and minds. Let's read it in Genesis 50:15-17.

¹⁵ And when Joseph's brethren saw that their father was dead, they said, Joseph will peradventure hate us, and will certainly requite us all the evil which we did unto him. ¹⁶ And they sent a messenger unto Joseph, saying, Thy father did command before he died, saying, ¹⁷ So shall ye say unto Joseph, Forgive, I pray thee now, the trespass of thy brethren, and their sin; for they did unto thee evil: and now, we pray thee, forgive the trespass of the servants of the God of thy father. And Joseph wept when they spake unto him.

These guys were scared. They were thinking that Joseph just pretended to be nice to them while Daddy was alive. Now that he was gone, they expected Joseph to be in the mood of revenge. They were begging for forgiveness. They wanted mercy. They didn't want what they deserved for what they did to their young brother.

When Joseph got the message, I believe that the brothers were close behind the messenger, and they were repentant. When he heard what they were saying, he was touched in his heart for them, realizing that they had been afraid of this moment for a long time.

- **Sin has a way of spoiling the enjoyment of life.**

- **We can choose to sin, but we cannot choose the consequences.**

Let's continue to read in verses 18-21.

> ^{18} *And his brethren also went and fell down before his face; and they said, Behold, we be thy servants.* ^{19} *And Joseph said unto them,* **Fear not: for am I in the place of God?** ^{20} *But as for you, ye thought evil against me; but God meant it unto good, to bring to pass, as it is this day, to save much people alive.* ^{21} *Now therefore fear ye not: I will nourish you, and your little ones. And he comforted them, and spake kindly unto them.*

Joseph's brothers bowed before him again as they had done so many times since they were reunited. Only this time, they were repentant. They were willing to be their little brother's servants. I am sure they remembered the telling of Joseph's dreams and how they had mocked him about those dreams. Now they knew that it was a God-given prophecy of what was to come.

- **Joseph is giving us a real example of true forgiveness.**

Joseph said to them, **"Fear not: for am I in the place of God?"** (v. 19)

The following is my dramatization of what Joseph might have said to his brothers.

"I am not God. I know that you were thinking evil against me, but God was in the plan. He turned the evil into good. He had a lot to teach me. He brought me to Egypt to put into action His plan to save many lives from hunger."

- **The Lord is teaching us through Joseph to save for the future, but most of all to totally maintain our faith in Him.**

Joseph knew that God would not want him to take revenge on his brothers. He knew that God was a merciful God, a caring God, a forgiving God. Joseph could not do anything but to forget the past and be in good fellowship with his repentant brothers. Also, an important thing here to remember is that, if he did not forgive them, what kind of testimony would that have been to the Egyptians? Joseph continued to speak comforting words to his ten brothers, nine of which, who had sold him as a slave.

Joseph had a substantial amount to be angry about. His brothers put him in a pit; he was sold as a slave; he was lied about by Mrs. Potiphar and he spent years in prison despite his innocence. All of this happened because of the hatred his brothers had against him. However, he did not get angry; he showed them love.

- **Love is an amazing emotion. The Bible says in *Proverbs 10:12, Hatred stirreth up strifes: but love covereth all sins.***

There are many more characteristics of love that you can read for yourself in 1 Corinthians 13. Joseph was loving and forgiving. We need to learn this. We need to be forgiving, especially when someone asks for compassion. If you are a Christian, if you know the Lord Jesus Christ as your Savior, then you are commanded by God to be forgiving. The Bible is full of verses that tell us to be forgiving. Let's read some of these verses. Luke 17:3-4.

> *³Take heed to yourselves: If thy brother trespass against thee, rebuke him; and if he repent,* **forgive** *him. ⁴And if he trespass against thee seven times in a day, and seven times in a day turn again to thee, saying, I repent; thou shalt* **forgive** *him.*

Now this is a hard thing to do. So, we need Jesus close to us. We need to be ready to forgive like Jesus wants us to forgive. Now let's read Matthew 18:21-22.

> *²¹ Then came Peter to him, and said,* **Lord, how oft shall my brother sin against me, and I forgive him? till seven times?** *²² Jesus saith unto him, I say not unto thee, Until seven times: but, Until seventy times seven.*

- Here is another question for this lesson.

"Lord, how oft shall my brother sin against me, and I forgive him? till seven times?"

I believe that Peter already knew about forgiving seven times in a day. Why did he then ask this question? Who knows? I am sure that he was surprised at the Lord's answer, *"I say not unto thee, Until seven times: but, Until seventy times seven."* Do the math of this statement. Yes, that is right—490. We are to forgive someone 490 times! I believe that before we get to 100 we will be in the habit of forgiving. We will be on the way to doing the Lord's will for our lives. Here is another verse to consider Ephesians 4:32.

And be ye kind one to another, tenderhearted, forgiving one another, even as God for Christ's sake hath forgiven you.

- **The way to be loving and forgiving is to stay close to the ONE WHO LOVES AND FORGIVES.**

Homework:

1. Memorize Luke 17:3-4 and Ephesians 4:32.

2. Look into your life and find that one person that you have not forgiven and forgive him or her. Call them. Write them a letter. Go see them if you are able. Write about the experience. What do you think it meant to the person to whom you offered forgiveness? Did they forgive you? How did you react? How does this make you feel now that you have made the effort to talk to this person?

NOTES

NOTES

NOTES

JONAH

CHAPTER 6

What Meanest Thou, O Sleeper?

Jonah 1:1-16

Now let's look at a preacher and see what questions we can find in his story.

> *¹Now the word of the Lord came unto Jonah the son of Amittai, saying, ² Arise, go to Nineveh, that great city, and cry against it; for their wickedness is come up before me.*

Jonah was commanded by God to preach to very wicked people. He told Jonah that He wanted them warned of their coming destruction. The Lord wanted them to have a chance to repent of their wicked ways as it says in 2 Peter 3:9.

> *The Lord is not slack concerning his promise, as some men count slackness; but is longsuffering to us-ward, not willing that any should perish, but that all should come to repentance.*

But Jonah had a better idea. At least he thought that it was better. Let's read verse 3,

³ But Jonah rose up to flee unto Tarshish from the presence of the Lord, and went down to Joppa; and he found a ship going to Tarshish: so he paid the fare thereof, and went down into it, to go with them unto Tarshish from the presence of the Lord.

Jonah began to make immediate plans to escape from the call of God on his life. He hoofed it to Joppa, running from the Lord. He was possibly thinking, "So far so good. Now I need to get a little farther away from the Lord just to make sure." When he got there, he paid for a ticket on a ship that was going to Tarshish. Now he thought that he was effectively avoiding the Lord God. He was confident that he was out of the reach of the all-present God. He was so confident that, when he boarded the ship, he went to SLEEP!

What he did not know was, while he was sleeping, the Lord, sent a horrible storm on the sea and the shipmates were afraid that they were going to die. They began to call upon their own gods to save them and began casting things out of the boat to lighten the load. Finally, someone realized that Jonah was not among them and went to look for him. Let's read verse 6.

*⁶ So the shipmaster came to him, and said unto him, **What meanest thou, O sleeper?** arise, call upon thy God, if so be that God will think upon us, that we perish not.*

The shipmaster was shocked that anyone could sleep through such a storm. Here is our question for this lesson.

- **"What meanest thou, O sleeper?"**

This man was appalled at Jonah. "Get up! What do you mean sleeping when we are all about to lose our lives? Call on your God to save us." Someone came up with an idea. They decided to cast lots. This is a method that was used many times in Bible times to determine an answer to their situation. Jonah was caught! He did not succeed in his attempt to run from the Lord. He was probably thinking, how can I get out of this situation? Now there came a tirade of questions from the men to Jonah in verse 8.

> *8 Then said they unto him, Tell us, we pray thee, for whose cause this evil is upon us; What is thine occupation? and whence comest thou? what is thy country? and of what people art thou?*

I can imagine that Jonah was thinking about telling them to slow down, not so many questions all at once, but Jonah remembered that they were all afraid for their lives. So he told the facts as they are in verses 9-10.

⁹And he said unto them, I am an Hebrew; and I fear the Lord, the God of heaven, which hath made the sea and the dry land. ¹⁰Then were the men exceedingly afraid, and said unto him. **Why hast thou done this?** *For the men knew that he fled from the presence of the Lord, because he had told them.*

Jonah opened up and told the men that presently, he feared the Lord God of Heaven, the One who made the earth, the oceans and all that you see. He told them that he was running away from this powerful God. He explained to them that the Lord wanted him to preach to a really wicked group of people. He said that he did not want to preach unto them the forgiveness of the Lord. I believe that Jonah had more fear of the Lord now than before he entered the ship. The men asked him,

"Why hast thou done this?" (v. 10)

I imagine that Jonah did not really realize that his running away would endanger anyone else. He just did not want to go to those wicked people and preach to them. He wanted them to perish in their sin.

- **We all need to remember that our sin affects others, our families, our friends, & those with whom we work.**

Now, let's not get ahead of the story. The shipmates wanted to know what to do to remedy the situation. Read verses 11-12.

¹¹ Then said they unto him, **What shall we do unto thee, that the sea may be calm unto us?** *for the sea wrought, and was tempestuous.* *¹² And he said unto them, Take me up, and cast me forth into the sea; so shall the sea be calm unto you: for I know that for my sake this great tempest is upon you.*

Now we have another question that is very significant. **"What shall we do unto thee, that the sea may be calm unto us?"** Jonah answered their question, "You have to throw me overboard to save your lives. It is my fault that you all are in this trouble. Just throw me overboard and your problems will be over."

I have often wondered about this situation. If Jonah really knew that he was the problem, why didn't he just jump into the sea and release these innocent men of their horrible fate? Then one day through reading, or listening to a sermon or just talking with my brilliant husband, I realized that the men needed to exhibit their faith in the God of creation, in Jonah's God in order to be saved. Of course, Jonah could have also been too afraid to jump in himself, thinking that it meant sure death.

Well, the men also thought that it would be sure death for Jonah, so they did the next best thing that they knew to do. Read verses 13-15.

^{13} Nevertheless the men rowed hard to bring it to the land; but they could not: for the sea wrought, and was tempestuous against them. ^{14} Wherefore they cried unto the Lord, and said, We beseech thee, O Lord, we beseech thee, let us not perish for this man's life, and lay not upon us innocent blood: for thou, O Lord, hast done as it pleased thee. ^{15} So they took up Jonah, and cast him forth into the sea: **and the sea ceased from her raging.**

The men tried to steer the ship to land, but that did not work. Then they cried out to God. I believe that they were very emotional in their crying out—they were desperate men. They were frenzied men! They did not want to die. They probably cried with loud voices, **"What do we do now?"** With that, they realized that they needed to do as Jonah had said and by faith throw him into the dangerous waters. Each man took an arm and a leg of Jonah. 1, 2, 3—into the raging water he sailed! The moment that they did it, the result amazed them. The sea settled into a sweet calm! The Creator had total control over the entire situation! Now read verse 16.

^{16} Then **the men feared the Lord exceedingly,** *and offered a sacrifice unto the Lord, and made vows.*

These men turned to the Lord. They gained a fear of the Lord that was right and just. These men realized who the real God of creation is. He has everything under control. They believed in the Creator.

Do you believe? Are you running from the Lord? Know that punishment will come if you are a child of the King.

- **You can't run from the Lord forever.**

If he has given you a calling, please go to Him now and get things into the right perspective. Ask the question, **"What do I do now?"** The Lord will answer you. He will give direction in your life. Think about the words in James 4 verse 8.

⁸ Draw nigh to God, and he will draw nigh to you. Cleanse your hands, ye sinners; and purify your hearts, ye double minded.

Homework:

1. Memorize 2 Peter 3:9 and James 4:8 Now don't tell me you are too old to memorize verses. You are never too old. So just do it. Don't tell me that you can't read well enough. Just get a recording of the verses and MEMORIZE THEM!

2. Write about your journey of fleeing from what God has called you to do. Jot down what steps you will take to carry out what God wants you to do.

NOTES

NOTES

CHAPTER 7

"Why Hast Thou Done This?"

Jonah 1:10 & 17-2:10

The last we saw of Jonah, he was being thrown overboard by the men in the ship. I imagine that Jonah's thoughts went something like this,

> *I sure hope death comes quickly. I never imagined that running from the Lord would cause me to end up in the bottom of the sea. Oh, why did I do all that running? Those men asked me a really good question.* **"Why hast thou done this?"** *(Jonah 1:10) Why did I do this? What was I thinking?*

- **No one can run from God and get away with it.**

This is the probable line of thinking that was quickly going through Jonah's mind when he was in the hands of the mariners and then flying through the air and finally splashing into the sea. Let's get on with the story. Read, please, Jonah 1:17.

*[17] Now **the Lord had prepared** a great fish to swallow up Jonah. And Jonah was in the belly of the fish three days and three nights.*

"The Lord had prepared ..." These are important words. Even though Jonah was a runaway preacher, the Lord was still right beside him waiting for him to listen. Not at all like he imagined He would be, but the Lord was there. He had everything under control. God is the Creator, so it was not hard for Him to prepare a big, big fish to swallow Jonah. Yuk—to be swallowed by a fish! This verse says that he was there in that yucky fish 3 days and 3 nights.

- **Do those numbers say anything to you?**

- **Yes, Jesus was in the grave for 3 days**

- **and 3 nights for our benefit.**

- **Jesus did no wrong.**

- **He was there for all of the people that had lived and**

- all that would live on this earth.

- He died for the sins of the whole world.

Ok let's get back to Jonah. Read, please, chapter 2:1.

> Then **Jonah prayed** *unto the*
> *Lord his God out of the fish's belly,*

Wow! Jonah prayed! Even though he disobeyed the Lord and ran from Him, the Lord was still his God.

- **Being a preacher, evangelist, or**
  teacher in the ministry of the Lord does
  not mean that we always do things right.

Sometimes the Lord has to bring us to a place where we will listen to Him, a place where there is total commitment to Him and to what He wants for our lives. I do believe that He had Jonah's attention, don't you? Now let's find out what Jonah said to the Lord in verse 2.

> *And said, I cried by reason of mine affliction unto the Lord,*
> *and* **he heard me***; out of the belly of hell cried I, and thou*
> *heardest my voice.*

Jonah was in a desperate situation. He was alive but in a horrible place. He realized that he needed help and he cried out to God for that help. Guess what? **The Lord heard him** and responded. Let's read more about what Jonah said in his prayer in verses 3-5.

> ³*For thou hadst cast me into the deep, in the midst of the seas; and the floods compassed me about: all thy billows and thy waves passed over me.* ⁴*Then I said, I am cast out of thy sight; yet I will look again toward thy holy temple.* ⁵*The waters compassed me about, even to the soul: the depth closed me round about, the weeds were wrapped about my head.*

Jonah was describing how it was when he was first cast into the sea. He was horrified by the enormous raging waters that surrounded him as he was thrown into the water. He felt the devastation of really being out of the Lord's sight. Yet he chose to look to the Almighty. Read verses 6-7.

> ⁶*I went down to the bottoms of the mountains; the earth with her bars was about me for ever: yet hast thou brought up my life from corruption, O Lord my God.* ⁷*When my soul fainted within me I remembered the Lord: and my prayer came in unto thee, into thine holy temple.*

Jonah acknowledged the Lord and prayed to Him from the fish's belly. He understood that his life was nothing without the Lord. Read verses 8-9.

⁸ They that observe lying vanities forsake their own mercy. ⁹ But I will sacrifice unto thee with the voice of thanksgiving; I will pay that that I have vowed. Salvation is of the Lord.

Now Jonah was saying thank you to the Lord from the depths of the sea and, worse yet, from the inside of a big fish that could swallow a man without breaking his bones or biting him. Jonah admitted that the only way out of his predicament was through the Lord. At that point the Lord gave instructions to the fish.

¹⁰ And the Lord spake unto the fish, and it vomited out Jonah upon the dry land.

We have something to learn here. When we realize that we are not in the Lord's will or worse yet, we are running from Him, all it takes is a prayer of admission to return to the Lord. Many times our detour from His perfect will may leave us with the marks of sin on our bodies and/or in our lives. We must use 1 John 1:9 as the Christian's bar of soap.

If we confess our sins, he is faithful and just to forgive us our sins, and to cleanse us from all unrighteousness.

If you are not serving the Lord but running from Him, before it is too late turn to Jesus and renew your fellowship with Him.

Homework:

1. Memorize 1 John 1:9.

2. Write about a time when you needed to return to the Lord, or write about how you need to return to the Lord's perfect for your life now.

NOTES

NOTES

CHAPTER 8

Who Can Tell If God Will Turn And Repent... That We Perish Not?

Jonah 3

Now Jonah stood on firm ground. The great fish that God had sent vomited him up onto the sandy shore. What do you think he looked like and smelled like? Yes, that is right! He smelled like a FISH! He had seaweed wrapped around him. His wet clothes clung to him. Slime from the fish's stomach dripped on him. He looked and smelled horrible! Now let's read chapter 3 verses 1-2.

> *¹And the word of the Lord came unto Jonah the second time, saying, ²Arise, go unto Nineveh, that great city, and preach unto it the preaching that I bid thee.*

Now the LORD was giving Jonah a second chance to obey Him. The LORD told Jonah to go to Nineveh, a very large city, and preach to the Ninevites all that the LORD wanted them to hear. It was clear that Jonah was to preach to those Ninevites. Now the question here is, "Will Jonah go this time to that very sinful city of Nineveh? Read now verses 3-4.

³ So Jonah arose, and went unto Nineveh, according to the word of the Lord. Now Nineveh was an exceeding great city of three days' journey. ⁴ And Jonah began to enter into the city a day's journey, and he cried, and said, Yet forty days, and Nineveh shall be overthrown.

Yes, Jonah obeyed the LORD and went to the city of Nineveh. This city was very large. It was so large that it would be a three day journey to walk all the way through the city. When Jonah entered the city he had traveled the distance of one day's walk and began to preach telling people that they had only forty days before judgment would come on them for their horrible sins. He repeated the same message everywhere he went in that massive city of Nineveh. Read verses 5-6.

*⁵ So **the people** of Nineveh **believed God,** and proclaimed a fast, and put on sackcloth, from the greatest of them even to the least of them. ⁶ For word came unto **the king of Nineveh,** and he arose from his throne, and he laid his robe from him, and **covered him with sackcloth, and sat in ashes.***

The rich and poor people of Nineveh, as well as the King of Nineveh, **believed God!** WOW! They called for a fast and put on sackcloth. Whether they were rich or poor they all wore sackcloth. In Bible times people wore sackcloth for clothes and put ashes on their heads if they were grieving or repentant. The whole city of Nineveh was repentant of their horrible sins. Even the king of Nineveh was repentant. The king actually wore sackcloth instead of his kingly garments. Read, please, verses 7-9.

⁷ And he caused it to be proclaimed and published through Nineveh by the decree of the king and his nobles, saying, Let neither man nor beast, herd nor flock, taste any thing: let them not feed, nor drink water: ⁸ But let man and beast be covered with sackcloth, and cry mightily unto God: yea, let them turn every one from his evil way, and from the violence that is in their hands. **⁹ Who can tell if God will turn and repent, and turn away from his fierce anger, that we perish not?**

The king commanded everyone in the city to fast. They were not to eat or drink anything. He also said that the animals were to do the same. They were to cry out to God, repenting of their evil deeds. Then the king asked the question for our lesson. **"Who can tell if God will turn and repent, and turn away from his fierce anger, that we perish not?"** The king wanted to know if God would change His mind about destroying the whole city of Nineveh, if they all repented. It appears that they were serious about repenting, because if not, God would not have done the following that is found in verse 10.

- **Remember, God knows our thoughts;**

- **He knows the whole truth,
  not just what people say.**

¹⁰ And God saw their works, that they turned from their evil way; and God repented of the evil, that he had said that he would do unto them; **and he did it not.**

God knew their hearts and that they had truly repented. Most of the time all we have to do is cry out to God and He will forgive us. I have said in the past that every time we call on the LORD, He will answer, but I have been reading repeatedly in Proverbs and in chapter 1 verses 23-25 it says:

²³ Turn you at my reproof: behold, I will pour out my spirit unto you, I will make known my words unto you. ²⁴ Because I have called, and ye refused; I have stretched out my hand, and no man regarded; ²⁵ But ye have set at nought all my counsel, and would none of my reproof:

Wisdom is talking. Wisdom wants to pour out the Words of God unto a receptive people. Wisdom called and was refused. Wisdom was ignored. The people would not take counsel or correction. There is a limit as to how long or how many opportunities a person will be afforded to respond to the Holy Spirit. Let's jump down to verses 28-29 of Proverbs 1.

²⁸ Then shall they call upon me, but I will not answer; they shall seek me early, but they shall not find me: ²⁹ For that they hated knowledge, and did not choose the fear of the Lord:

There comes a time when you get a last chance at repenting. Some will call but will get no answer because it is too late.

- **Why is it too late?**

- **Because they hated knowledge and did not choose the fear of the LORD:**

Don't wait too long. Accept the salvation of the Lord now before it is too late. The Spirit will not always be ready to convict. Don't wait too long. There is a promise in Proverbs 1:33

³³ But whoso hearkeneth unto me shall dwell safely, and shall be quiet from fear of evil.

- **Be safe with the LORD!**

Homework:

1. Memorize Proverbs 1:28-29 and verse 33.

2. Write about a time when you realized that you needed to repent, to turn around and follow Jesus.

NOTES

NOTES

CHAPTER 9

Was Not This My Saying, When I Was Yet In My Country?

Jonah 4

All the people of Nineveh repented in our last lesson. What a blessing that would be to see the people in an entire city repent! However, there was one that was not at all happy. Who do you think it was? Yep! It was Jonah. Let's begin reading in chapter 4 verse 1.

> *¹But it displeased Jonah exceedingly, and he was very angry.* *²And he prayed unto the Lord, and said, I pray thee, O Lord,* **was not this my saying, when I was yet in my country?** *Therefore I fled before unto Tarshish: for I knew that thou art a gracious God, and merciful, slow to anger, and of great kindness, and repentest thee of the evil.* *³Therefore now, O Lord, take, I beseech thee, my life from me; for it is better for me to die than to live.*

Jonah was furious! He spoke especially hatefully to the Lord. I cannot imagine talking to the Lord in the manner that Jonah did. Jonah said, *"**Was not this my saying, when I was yet in my country?** You, Lord,* are too kind and forgiving. It takes you a long time to get angry. I knew that you would not destroy these people. I might as well die. Just kill me right here and now. You can do it. So just kill me and get it over with!"

My question for Jonah is, "Why is it necessary for you to die? What good would that do? The Ninevites probably would not even know about your death anyway." He was just mad at God and wanted God to kill him. It was like a kid that didn't get his way and said, "I am going to eat some worms and die." Again this is crazy. Most of the people in Nineveh would think that the preacher had just left to go to another city and preach. So here we have a preacher angry with God, because the people repented and the Lord spared their lives. Aren't we as Christians supposed to be happy when people turn to the Lord? Yes, of course, we are. Well, let's see what happens next. Read verses 4-8.

*⁴ Then said the Lord, **Doest thou well to be angry?** ⁵ So Jonah went out of the city, and sat on the east side of the city, and there made him a booth, and sat under it in the shadow, till he might see what would become of the city. ⁶ And the Lord God prepared a gourd, and made it to come up over Jonah, that it might be a shadow over his head, to deliver him from his grief. So Jonah was exceeding glad of the gourd. ⁷ But God prepared a worm when the morning rose the next day, and it smote the gourd that it withered. ⁸ And it came to pass, when the sun did arise, that God prepared a vehement east* *wind; and the sun beat upon the head of Jonah, that he fainted, and wished in himself to die, and said, It is better for me to die than to live.*

The Lord had His own question for Jonah. "Are you right in being angry?" Jonah made no comment or answer to the Lord's question. He walked out, made himself a shelter and sat to watch and see if the Lord would really destroy the city of Nineveh. The Lord put Jonah to the test. He caused a gourd to grow up to give shade to Jonah. This made the angry preacher happy. Then the next day the Lord sent a worm to eat the plant and it withered and died. Then the Lord sent a strong hot wind, causing the sun to beat down onto Jonah's head. Again we hear Jonah wishing for death. The preacher was depressed and thought nothing was going right for him so he might as well die. Now the Lord had another question for Jonah. Let's read verses 9-11.

*⁹ And God said to Jonah, **Doest thou well to be angry for the gourd?** And he said, I do well to be angry, even unto death. ¹⁰ Then said the Lord, Thou hast had pity on the gourd, for the which thou hast not laboured, neither madest it grow; which came up in a night, and perished in a night: ¹¹ And should not I spare Nineveh, that great city, wherein are more than sixscore thousand persons that cannot discern between their right hand and their left hand; and also much cattle?*

God asked Jonah, "Are you right for being angry because the plant died?" Jonah said that he had a right to be angry because it gave him shade. He was so angry that he wanted to die.

The Lord explained to Jonah that he did not work to plant the gourd and he did not make it grow. In other words, it was not his to be angry about. The gourd thrived one day and withered the next. Just think about all those people in Nineveh. There were 120,000 people that did not know their right hand from their left. Aren't they of much more importance than a simple plant that was only alive for one day?

What can we learn from this?

1. The Lord knows more than we do.

2. He knew about the people in Nineveh and knew their problems.

3. He is a caring, loving and forgiving God.

4. He wants all to come to repentance. Let's read 2 Peter 3:9.

The Lord is not slack concerning his promise, as some men count slackness; but is longsuffering to us-ward, not willing that any should perish, but that all should come to repentance.

This verse proves that the Lord wants all to be saved.

My son, Eric, is a preacher. He preaches the way of salvation to the ones who come to church and to those we meet when we go door knocking. **If** he were like Jonah, he would be mad if a man told him,

"Pastor Eric, I want to be saved. I want to live for Jesus. In fact I believe that Jesus died in my place. I accept His sacrifice for me." Do you think that Pastor Eric would come home angry that a man accepted the Lord?

NO! NO! NO!
Eric would be so HAPPY!
Satan lost one soul and THE LORD GAINED ONE SOUL!
ERIC WOULD BE PRAISING THE LORD!

So many times, I hear people say that there is no way that their family member will ever change. I tell them that our Lord is the God of miracles. He can change the heart of anyone for whom we pray. We should expect God to answer our prayers. We need to remember 1 John 5:14-15.

> *And this is the confidence that we have in him, that, if we ask any thing according to his will, he heareth us:* [15] *And if we know that he hear us, whatsoever we ask, we know that we have the petitions that we desired of him.*

- **The Lord wants people to be saved. This is His will.**

- **Therefore, we need to pray expecting our loved ones to repent.**

Homework:

1. Memorize 2 Peter 3:9 and 1 John 5:14-15.

2. Write about what you have learned and how it applies to you.

NOTES

NOTES

CHAPTER 10

Conclusion

We have studied about Joseph in this book. Joseph never gave up on serving his Lord, even though he was hated by his brothers. Nine of his brothers sold him as a slave. While in Egypt he became the best worker that he could be. His owner rewarded him with the responsibility of all of his possessions. Then Mrs. Potipher lied about him. Joseph was thrown into prison. Continuing to trust in the God of Heaven, Joseph became the best prisoner that had ever been incarcerated. He was a person that helped others. He interpreted the dreams of two men but the one that lived did not keep his promise to Joseph, but forgot him. Do you think that all of this made Joseph happy? No! However, it did not make him rebellious. He still served the Lord the best way that he could in his circumstances. The Lord God of Heaven rewarded his faithfulness. He put him into a place of authority and blessed him with a wife and two sons, and finally he was blessed to see his father and brothers again.

- **We cannot put a time restraint on our service to the Lord God of Heaven.**

- **We need to serve Him daily no matter what happens.**

We also studied about Jonah. However, all we know about Jonah is one time that he ran away from God. The God of Heaven told him to preach to the people in Nineveh. He was afraid of the people of Nineveh. He did not want them to be saved. He thought they deserved punishment.

What have we learned from this man's actions?

1. We can't successfully run away from God. God knows all and sees all.

2. We need to be obedient to the Lord.

3. We need to remember that all people need the opportunity to repent.

4. We need to fear the Lord, not people and circumstances.

5. We need to remember that we all deserve punishment.

6. It is only through the love and mercy of the Lord that we have salvation.

Re-read this book slowly and study the Bible account of these men. Ask the Lord to guide you in the study. He will. "If we ask anything according to His will He heareth us."

God bless you one and all,
Sarah Jane Conaway
sarahjane@auntjane.ws

Let me hear from you my readers. If you have any question, just email me and we will either chat via email or set up a time to talk on the phone.

About the Author

Sarah Jane has been a Christian for over 56 years. In that time she has taught Sunday school, ladies classes, classes on how to teach Sunday school and counseled ladies. She has also spoken to ladies groups and churches about her ministry. She taught her three sons their schooling using Accelerated Christian Education. On the mission field in Papua New Guinea she had a school for the nationals from 1988–1993. She has also taught missionary children in Mexico.

She and her husband, Ron, and their sons began their missionary journey with deputation in January 1978. In 1980 they arrived in Papua New Guinea and began learning the language in order to share the Gospel with the New Guineans. Their ministry moved to Mexico in 1995 where they are currently ministering. Ron graduated to Heaven in January 2005. She and two of her three sons have continued the ministry.

She followed the Lord's leading in March of 2015 beginning her career as an author.

You can contact her at sarahjane@auntjane.ws. You can also visit her website: www.auntjane.ws

Acknowledgements

I want to say thank you to Chandler Bolt and Sean Sumner of Self Publishing School for all of the help you have given me in getting this second book done.

Thanks also goes to two of my sons, Eric and Timothy, who are here with me for helping me get things done that I had a difficult time understanding, as well as for the encouragement given.

Thank you to Terry and Karen Milligan, who so patiently edited my book and explained things to me.

I want to give my thanks to my niece Sarah Lynne Conaway for the art work done on the book cover. It makes me happy for you to have a part in the publication of this book.

Also I want to thank all of my supporters who have prayed for me in my new ministry as an author.

Now It Is Your Turn!

Self Publish your book with
www.Self-PublishingSchool.com

Just tell them that Sarah Jane Conaway
sent you and you will receive a $250 discount

www.ingramcontent.com/pod-product-compliance
Lightning Source LLC
Chambersburg PA
CBHW021207020426
42331CB00003B/242